The Oceans and Coral

Coloured Version

CHILDREN SAVING OUR PLANET SERIES

CAROL SUTTERS

AuthorHouse™ UK
1663 Liberty Drive
Bloomington, IN 47403 USA
www.authorhouse.co.uk
UK TFN: 0800 0148641 (Toll Free inside the UK)
UK Local: 02036 956322 (+44 20 3695 6322 from outside the UK)

Because of the dynamic nature of the Internet, any web addresses or links contained in this book may have changed since publication and may no longer be valid. The views expressed in this work are solely those of the author and do not necessarily reflect the views of the publisher, and the publisher hereby disclaims any responsibility for them.

Any people depicted in stock imagery provided by Getty Images are models, and such images are being used for illustrative purposes only. Certain stock imagery © Getty Images.

This book is printed on acid-free paper.

ISBN: 978-1-6655-8795-2 (sc)
ISBN: 978-1-6655-8796-9 (e)

Library of Congress Control Number: 2021907311

Print information available on the last page.

Published by AuthorHouse 04/19/2021

authorHOUSE®

During their seaside holiday, Tom and Kate became very interested in the damage humans are doing to sea animals by us leaving waste plastic rubbish in or near the seaside. When they returned home to their gran's, they asked her for more information about the ocean and whether humans were destroying these?

In response gran suggested, *"I think we should all watch a programme about the deep seas and oceans."* They started watching about the Australian Great Barrier Coral Reef.

"What is a Coral reef?" asks Tom.

Coral Polyps

"*There are many coral reefs,*" replies Mum. "*The biggest and most famous is the Great Barrier Coral Reef in the Pacific Ocean. It is off the coast of Queensland on the East Coast of Australia. It is made up of over 2,900 reefs over 900 islands. It supports over 1600 species of fish.*"

The television programme explained the background to coral.

Polyps

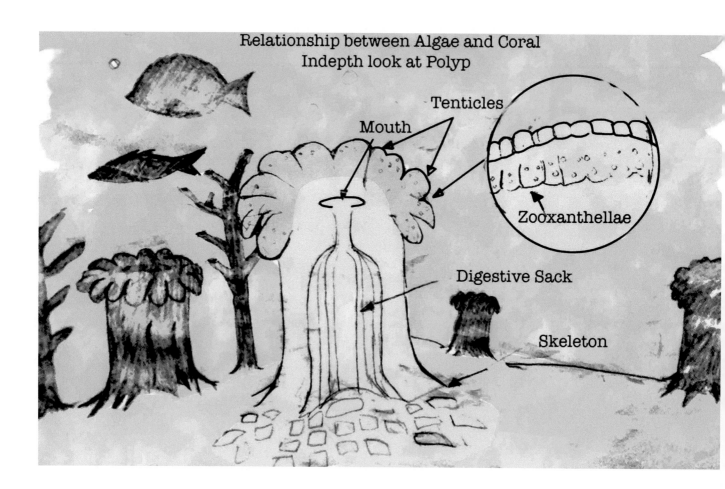

Relationship between Algae and Coral
Indepth look at Polyp

Tenticles

Mouth

Zooxanthellae

Digestive Sack

Skeleton

Coral polyps are like jelly fish or sea anemones. They are very simple animals that form a hard base and attach themselves to the rock on the sea bed. Polyps multiply into thousands of polyps. Simple tiny microscopic plants called algae live inside the polyp cells. Corals are bright and colourful because of these microscopic algae called zooxanthellae that live within them. The algae capture the energy from sunlight and they provide nutrients or food for the polyps to live. The algae produce oxygen and help to remove waste. So the algae and polyps live in harmony together. This is a mutually beneficial relationship. Corals would not survive without the microscopic algae inside them.

There are many different colours of coral reefs and they can be very beautiful. Some are fluorescent. The colour depends on the photosynthetic algae inside them. Coral colours can be green, brown, pink, yellow, red, purple and blue.

Tom and Kate see the beautiful colours on the television programme. It shows that the Great Barrier Reef looking blue-green as the water filters out other colours.

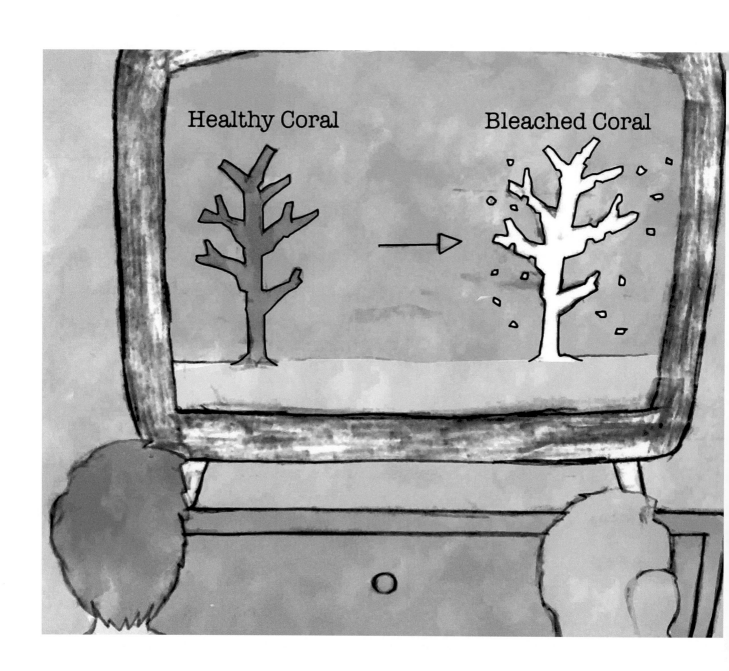

When coral is bleached the coral expels the algae and most corals die as they do not have enough time to recover between bleaching events. This means fish and algae lose a source of energy and food. The programme said the leading cause of bleaching corals is an increase in the water temperature, which is likely to be the result of human actions. Coral reefs are expected to experience many more beaching events due to high temperatures before 2040. Coral reefs are dying across the world and action must be taken to prevent this. It is estimated about a quarter of the Great Barrier Reef has died in the last few years.

There are other causes of bleaching as well which we humans are responsible for, and these include:

- Over or excessive fishing increasing zooplankton area.
- Herbicides or weed killers.
- High sea levels caused by global warming.
- Mineral dust from Africa caused by droughts.
- Chemical and oil spillage from tankers.
- Pollutants such as human skin sunscreens.
- Making the seas more acidic with pollutants such as increased carbon dioxide levels in the air, which dissolves in seawater.

When seas become more acidic, it makes the corals more porous as the acidic water corrodes the skeleton-like structure of corals. This makes it more likely to break. The coral reef is the architecture that provides an ecosystem for thousands of species. It is a shelter for many animals including fish, sharks, jellyfish, sea anemones, crabs, sponges, sea turtles, shrimps and many others. Corals provide shelter from predators and support organisms at the base of the ocean food chain. If reef systems collapse some already threatened species could become extinct. Coral reefs support some of the most biodiverse ecosystems on the planet.

"Why is this important?" questions Tom "It changes the natural environment called the ecosystem in which these off shore corals, algae and other small fish live," says mum. "These animals and plants live by feeding from each other and when their natural ecosystem is changed many of them die. Many coral reef fish die when the temperature of the water increases slightly. The whole of the seas and oceans are threatened by the loss of corals. Coral reefs support coastal shorelines against waves, storms and floods, which helps prevent loss of human life and property. The reefs also provide jobs and recreation for local people. It is estimated that half a billion people depend on coral reefs for food, income and protection."

What did we learn today? (tick the box if you understood and agree)

☐ Corals are animals which live with microscopic algae inside them giving them colour. Healthy coral is green, brown and colourful, not bleached.

☐ Coral reefs provide a complex ecosystem for many fish and other sea creatures to live in.

☐ Coral reefs produce much needed oxygen for species in deep oceans to survive.

☐ The whole marine ocean ecosystem of the world is threatened if we destroy coral reefs.

☐ Factors that kill coral reefs include increasing the temperature of the oceans, acidifying the water, coral bleaching, over fishing and others.

☐ Children can act together to tackle both the climate and biodiversity emergency in coral reefs. This will help us to save the planet.

Find out what Kate and Tom learn about Our Carbon Footprint in book 11.

Children Saving our Planet Series

Books

1. **Tom and Kate Go to Westminster**

2. **Kate and Tom Learn About Fossil Fuels**

3. **Tom and Kate Chose Green Carbon**

4. **Tress and Deforestation**

5. **Our Neighbourhood Houses**

6. **Our Neighbourhood Roads**

7. **Shopping at the Farm Shop**

8. **Travelling to a Holiday by the Sea**

9. **Picnic at the Seaside on Holiday**

These series of simple books explain the landmark importance of Children's participation in the Extinction rebellion protest. Children actively want to encourage and support adults to urgently tackle both the Climate and the Biodiversity emergencies. The booklets enable children at an early age to understand some of the scientific principles that are affecting the destruction of the planet. If global political and economic systems fail to address the climate emergency, the responsibility will rest upon children to save the Planet for themselves.

This series is dedicated to

Theodore, Aria and Ophelia.

Printed in the United States
by Baker & Taylor Publisher Services